Yours To Know

Yours To Know

Poems and Rhymes

FREN THOMPSON

Debony Production

ISBN-13: 978-0-9792150-7-0
ISBN-10: 0-9792150-7-2

DEDICATION

To my wife

and daughter

my late mother

and late father

All from whom I was inspired

MUCH LOVE!!

ACKNOWLEDGEMENTS

The author expresses appreciation to
Lorraine Thompson and Maxine Gibbs
who contributed their literary and
editorial skills to the compilation of
this book
and to
Nia Gibbs who developed the illustration
for the book cover

PREFACE

Through the years poetry has been used to console, to inspire, and to woo. In many cases they have left a permanent imprint on our minds.

I hope that the verses in this book contribute to the development of feelings and desires that impact the world in a positive way.

INTRODUCTION

In our daily lives we strive to accomplish many things. We experience situations which test our knowledge, strength and resilience. We encounter challenges, setbacks and failure. We also succeed in some things and learn and grow as we advance in life.

This collection of poems and rhymes contains verses which each make a specific statement about an experience, topic or feeling. These topics include love, kindness, hope, awareness, greed and selfishness. Each verse gives insight into, and provides true meaning to, these topics. They can be easily remembered and retained as life lessons to guide us in responding to relevant situations.

1

We watch the sun rise in the east

And journey a long way to the west

Like a magic wand that was spun

We wonder how that was really done

We know not of all things nature has to do

For nature has its secrets too

2

How does the air we breathe evolve?

What causes the wind we feel to appear?

These are things we can't do without

And these we know little about

The air we breathe is given free

And so is the wind that we feel

They are mysteries that will always be

3

Come outside and have some fun

Enjoy the breeze and the morning sun

Bask in the fresh air and calm that abide

All of which nature greatly provide

These are gifts that we were given

To make our lives worth livin'

We should keep these wonders together

So they won't be lost forever

4

The moon glowing in the sky

With shining stars flickering by

We gape in awe and ponder

How nature created such wonder

5

I made a garden in my yard

With lots of flowers and edible things

I have had so many rewards

And enjoy the beauty that it brings

It's great at times for me to relax and watch

The butterflies, bees and birds it attracts

All these things nature provides

To my garden in my yard

6

When our flowers start to bloom

They take away all our gloom

We have such joy for hours

From their lovely smell and various colors

7

We do some things for our pleasure

Some we must, some at our leisure

Gardening some of us like to do

Others like music, writing, and reading too

Whatever choice you might make

You will find lots of real pleasure

Just doing things at your own leisure

8

I make a lot of various toys

For kids to play with and enjoy

It's a good thing I have done

So I can sit and watch the kids have fun

With satisfaction and a real big smile

I enjoy doing it all the while

9

I am a man that always strive

To help people advance and survive

What I have I will kindly give

So that others can be able to live

10

Do good to others, the righteous man said

Blessing from heaven you will be paid

For all the love and kindness you give

The world will be better for all to live

Goodness is in everyone's soul

We must share it with the whole wide world

11

Pray for me, the lonely man asked

I need love and happiness in my heart

If you believe prayers will help

Why not pray for yourself and others as well?

I will also pray for you and for others

12

I pray before going to bed

And pray as I awake

Praying is now a part of me

It seems to rule my destiny

13

Love will often be expressed by some

And others are afraid of being bitten

For them it's all or none

Love is in the heart of everyone

Love is still our best gift given

FREN THOMPSON

14

Some will use love to deceive

To misuse, control and mislead

No matter what they say or do

Our love they do still receive

15

Love that's given or taken

Will remain in the hearts of everyone

Both the giver and the taker

Will have love in their hearts awaken

16

True love that we have we should cherish

And nurture, grow, and nourish

We should honor, respect, and care

For it is dear

The gift of love we were given

Should make us all driven

Not only just today

But each and every day

17

A young girl in haste to marry

She seeks true love in a hurry

She doesn't know what lies ahead

For dubious ones are at the ready

To goad and steer her to their bed

By telling her things she likes to hear

She can be fooled and easily led

Wait awhile don't be in despair my dear

Unlike the beginning, at the end

You will find a faithful friend

18

Everyone should have a friend

To trust, to love, and to defend

With pride and honor we should share

With a friend that we hold dear

19

With crave and longing young girls aspire

To find true love and all its pleasure

A mother sensing her daughters' desire

Counselled her on things she should know

Wait awhile for tomorrow, she said

Today will be gone but tomorrow will come

As you grow you will become smarter

And then know that tomorrow is forever

20

We learn at first how to crawl

Then we learn how to walk

Soon we start to walk upright

And to laugh and also talk

By doing the things that we learn

We should be able to do things right

21

A man without love is a man all alone

He knows not what to look for

Or what is there to see

He relishes in past memories

That will never fulfill his longings

Awake my friend, look for love

It's there waiting for everyone

22

Love we feel and we express

To those that we do accept

To some it's given only now; to others, never

But love should be given forever

23

On branches doves sit and coo

To attract mates and to woo

Soon each finds a capable wife

And begins to mate for life

24

Bestowed on all is the gift of goodness

To fulfill a mission of love and compassion

Some will be quick to respond and care

To help the sick and those in despair

Goodness comes in every form

For us to act on and to perform

25

Take my hand, the blind man said

It's very dark and the path is dim

I need to get home so I can rest

Thanks for being so willing to assist

May the goodness in you remain your asset

26

Men can do a lot of good

For all to live as they should

Giving up ones' selfish desire

Will allow giving to others what they desire

27

A baby born into this great world

With raw innocence that's unknown

A mothers' love and deep devotion

She cuddles her babe with fierce protection

A father looks on with great admiration

But a mothers' care is total dedication

Mother and child become so attached

Father can only sit and watch

Both parents lend to their baby's growth

With lots of love and tender care

Blessing from above they pray

That they may have each other every day

28

Give me peace upon this earth

So I can enjoy what it is worth

Love, blessing, and joy is my wish

In beauty that surrounds us all

That is how I will have a ball

29

We were given a great big world

Free of smog and air pollution

In search of oil, coal, and gold

Men have caused much destruction

Leaving the earth with so much void

Nuclear weapons can easily be found

In many countries stored underground

Good we can do, as we should

To make this world much better

For some profiteering gives financial gain

But for others a clean safe world is their one and only aim

Not the good that just leaves us spellbound

30

Men were given the tools to advance

But some refrain from ever taking the chance

They always take the easy way out

That stifles chances for better growth

31

In the Fall leaves fall from a tree

Then the tree renews itself for better growth

If a tree can shed its unwanted leaves

Why can't men drop their selfish ideals

And grow new strength for a better world

Nature shows us good ways to develop

But some men refuse to learn and follow

The example that simple trees allow

32

Some people have a very big head

And in it a very small brain

Using their head to only wear a hat

And their brain for ill-gotten gain

Doing odd things, heaven knows what

That will only bring them shame

33

Men do some very bad things

Not caring whether it is sin

They do these things for mere greed

No matter where it may lead

34

A young boy likes to fly his kite

And watch it soar at different heights

In the wind that he can never see

His kite floats to and fro with ease

Oh what magic nature provides

It gives us things we can enjoy

A young boy with kite in the sky at play

An adult enjoys walks on a sunny day

Nature has given us all we need

To live our lives any way we feel

35

Summer is a time for fun

To be outdoors and enjoy the sun

And do things at your own behest

That you feel suits you best

36

Dead and gone are those departed

Leaving behind many brokenhearted

Heaven or hell they go, or not

It's their secret, we won't know that

37

We mourn our dead and lay them to rest

But in our hearts won't let them die

In our minds and thoughts they lie

It's as if they are here with us

We just have to live and learn

They will never ever return

38

Family and friends who died before us

Have left us wondering where they go

It's a secret we won't know

No one has ever returned to tell us

Where they go and what they do

39

Let us pray for our dead

So they may enter with grace

Their rightful place in a grave

We know where they had lived

Not where they are now going

40

We went to church for holiness

But out we came with emptiness

In we went expecting something

Out we came with only nothing

41

Helping those in dire need

Is real kindness that you concede

It frees you from inner greed

And helps someone else to succeed

42

Some people use others to get to the top

Instead of a ladder to reach their goal

In getting there they should be told

Be sure to do good for behold

The fall can be very hard if you drop

43

Greed will always make some men rich

By hoarding all that they receive

They never care to share or make gifts

To those that really need lifts

44

We were showered with blessings from above

To care and share with all our love

Some men think it should be only for them

That blessings should really be spent

They will lie and steal to any length

To prevent anyone else from having a cent

All mankind should have a share

For a better life each and every day

45

We are given a world to live in

With all the things we need to exist

It's big enough for us to share

To love each other and coexist

But some men don't seem to care

They plot many ways to take it all

Leaving some with none at all

Some were elected to lead and rule

But they treat us as if we are fools

Let's think of each other, give a heart

For we might lose what's given

If we are not very smart

46

Why can't men learn from a dove

To show concern and to love

Do the things that are right

Instead of showing their might

47

Hope is lost when things go bad

They get us down and we feel real sad

Think of good moments, have happy thoughts

That can fill your heart with joy

Hope can easily be restored

If good we can do is explored

Put aside those selfish ploys

Let's surround ourselves with love and pride

And do our good that has been stored

48

When trouble ails and causes doom

It brings along sadness and gloom

Remember him the Prince Of Peace

Who taught us love with so much grace

Let His spirit fill the empty space

With love and hope to do us good

49

A poor man strives in vain to succeed

To make a living and ease his pain

Though heavy his tasks to fill his needs

With love and care he does good deeds

All he needs is a chance to excel

To keep him from living in total hell

This wish he made for men to be

Free and happy and live well

50

The righteous man condemns a sinner

He prides himself as a saintly soul

That is cleansed from sin deep within

Righteous he may be today, a sinner tomorrow

He sits on someone's tomb and feels no sorrow

51

What I got from this world I share

To free the poor from despair

Bless your soul, someone said in earnest

Thanks a lot for all your kindness

Blessed am I with what I have

And to share with others is divine

So blessed I am to give, I replied

52

With cup in hand a blind man peddle

To try to fill his empty belly

Another man in a suit and quite able

Tries to build his selfish gain

Why am I not getting a dole, he asked

We only help those in need

Not the greedy, someone remarked

53

If your thoughts are sad and low

Take some time to make them glow

Think of good times you have had

Good times you can once again have

54

We can make ourselves happy or sad

By remembering good or bad times we have had

Good memories will always overshadow the bad

Forget the past and what is lost

Try to be happy at all cost

You just don't know what will happen next

55

Faced with many different views

Some are false and some are true too

Truth and falsity are all well made

All of which are in the news

Maybe at times we might be confused

So when you doubt what to do

Use your head to find the fact

And not to only wear a hat

56

History has played a great big part

In changing mans' life and decisions too

Embrace the good we learn from it

And avoid the wrong that did exist

To credit history for repeating itself

Is a fable and an excuse we use

Men are the ones repeating history

57

When similar things from the past appear

Men often seem to be prepared

To use the term that suits them best

That history has repeated itself

But in fact that's not so true

Without thinking, or for gain, or for fame

Man himself has repeated history

©Tinylessonsblog

58

Our neighbor once was our beloved friend

We shared our love and traded gifts

Soon love was lost and hate set in

And war broke out with iron fists

Lives were lost among other things

With sadness and despair that it brings

Why can't we care and together exist

59

Men were given an enormous gift

To build and care for a life worth living

Together we all did good things

We shared knowledge and many ideas

To bring out the best of mans' being

Then power and greed set in

Man pursued his selfish desire

Now it's to each his own

Himself is first

It's only me and I together

60

In times of crisis we all belong

Joined together as if one

Oh what joy to see such unity

Without the threat of mutiny

Love once more is lost from our way

That leads us to many a bad day

Caring and sharing have now all gone

And some just say others don't belong

61

When disaster struck men seemed to care

They joined together and lent a hand

Like one family they faced the challenge

And came as one to repair the damage

Tasks well done they saluted and gave cheer

For the good they had done amid despair

Normalcy has now returned

And forgotten

Is all the good begotten

It's once more me and I

Those and them

And you for yourself

62

A man will lure others to his way

Like a spiders' great big web can do

You are trapped by talk so kindly given

That's a ploy he has well woven

To have you think and act like him

When caught up in mans' web or net

Trapped you are in his ploy and whim

Avoid the bait that seems to attract

Be ready for any fatal attack

Give good thought to what seems best

So you will always pass the test

63

Men take an oath to serve with pride

An oath that is made for them to abide

Raise your hand and swear to God above

To tell the truth is what you vow

To do always, not just now

Men have lied when asked to comply

They show disdain for their oath, they just lie

To them their vows do not apply

Are these men to carry our banner

When they show such disrespect and dishonor?

64

Some will tell you what's not true

Just to have you join their crew

Be leery of what they say and do

Think it over and use your head

You should decide on your own fate instead

Before it's just too late for you

To your own self be true

Trust in the right that you must do

Don't be led by those who lied

Maintain your dignity, honor, and pride

65

Leaders lie and deceive their followers

To have a stronghold and to control

Not having any pride or honor to uphold

They feel free to have their own way

They say things followers want to hear

Things with no true meaning followers can hold dear

It doesn't matter what lies followers are told

They stay devoted in a leaders' fold

66

People are from different nations

But they have evolved ever since creation

Some will speak in a different tongue

Depending on where they live or come from

All people are still one creation

Even if they are all not from one nation

67

Nations will explore and exploit each other

Even make wars that cause harm and sorrow

To maim and kill their very own brother

Never stopping to care where, what, or who

Or that their brothers are really humans too

68

We go to church and kneel and pray

To hope and wish for better days

We ask for peace and love in Gods' name

While others ask for wealth and fame

Some will even pose as heavenly hosts

To earn ones' trust for financial gain

Good prayers should always be done

So blessings will be granted from above

69

A pastor filled with hate and distrust

Professed love and honesty to his followers

Love, he said, is for all to share

And honesty lies in everyone that cares

Doubtful of his truth and devotion

Someone posed this valid question

How can you preach love and honesty to us

When you do not embrace it

It's a fact you are here to deceive

Not one word you say we believe

70

Making a fool of someone

Does not really make them a fool

Some people will always break the rule

And make a fool of everyone

Deceiving someone is dishonest

And to make a fool of anyone

Means you are a dishonest person

71

Measure me with honesty

Not with weakness

Measure me with kindness

Not with stupidity

A man is measured by his deeds

I am a man so possessed indeed

72

Call me fraternizing

But I am only friendly

Call me compromising

But I am only considerate

What am I, if I am not these things

Just a lonely man crying

For friendship, love, and happiness

73

We are given the morning sun

Family and friends to love and care

The gift of a new day to share

Peace and happiness for everyone

74

Take some time to choose a friend

Not just at their desire

Tall or short might be your quest

Small in stature, or large in quality is another test

Measure them with truth and honesty

Your choice should always be for the best

To have a good friend is what you need in the end

75

As a teen I would always stray

From what my parents would say

I did not know then what I now know

As an adult now on my own

Lessons taught and lessons learned

Make for knowledge well earned

76

Children go to prep school and college

To improve their lives

And to acquire knowledge

In they went, untrained and vague

Out they came, well trained and prepared

Now empowered with advanced education

What they do with it is the question

77

As we look toward the sky

We explore the planets so high

To try and find what's in those worlds

How many they are, where they lie

As they appear in the sky

78

Planet earth we were given

For everyone to care and to share

Some took charge and were driven

To take it all and not to share

79

A dog they say is mans' best friend

But why as a man

Am I not so acclaimed

A dog will growl for his food

For water, and at you too

A dog will whine to go for walks

And sometimes to just be left alone

While a man is always prone

To give of self

To love, to share

Why am I not mans' best friend

80

Pets are smart and brainy too

They adapt and know to manipulate us too

We know these things our pets will do

Yet they remain our family friend

To share our love to the very end

And to amuse us like some humans do

81

Come under the sheet with me my sweet

To warm your body and cold feet

With bodies meshed as if we are one

We'll fall asleep spent and worn

When morning comes with heavenly bliss

We'll greet each other with a kiss

And with our bodies still entwined

We hope it won't be hard to then unwind

82

My lovely maiden clear your head

You can freely take my just-made bed

If you are sure and extremely willing

To make love that's slow and fulfilling

You will find it to be quite thrilling

83

A house is mans' castle

Where he pleases himself at his leisure

Doing all he wants for his pleasure

And never seems to be rattled

By anything that mars his desire

84

You get home from working hard today

And head for your favorite room

To take away weariness, sadness, and gloom

From the hectic, long, tiresome day

Your favorite room in which you can now stay

85

The chair in which we often sit

Never seems to care or resist

It accommodates us with such ease

All we do is just sit and laze

86

The falcon nests high on a hill

And soars far above in the sky

Looking up it seems so high

There the billy goat roams at will

Never afraid or seemingly shy

Looking at them gives us such a thrill

87

We hear the thunder in the sky

And see the lightning going by

We will often wonder just how

We always see the lightning flash

But never see the thunder roll

88

At times the sky is always all one color blue

And at times it has multiple hues of blue

Colors, shapes, and forms of hues they appear

Thanks to the sky for being right there

89

The turn of day into night

Gives us time to rest and replenish

To sleep and dream of heaven knows what

Then to wake at dawns' first rising

And find that night has turned to day

90

I had a dream that seemed so real

That had great hope and appeal

Of all the things, this dream I wanted to keep

But I awoke to find it was a vision in my sleep

Real or not, I know now

It was just a dream that I had in tow

91

Leaders tend to have their way

To have their people obey

They will steal, cheat, and lie

In ways to have everyone abide

92

A selfish man with his estate

Builds a fence and a gate

He securely shuts himself in

While keeping everyone else out

That's his way of feeling safe

Living in his great estate

93

Good news we always like to hear

To brighten us with pleasant cheer

Happy times we should really preserve

They give us loving moments we deserve

94

Doctors work to heal the sick

To treat their many ailment

The sick respond to their good treatment

Once again to be feeling fit

95

Walking along the beach I find

Seems to help my health and mind

To sink my feet into the sand

And even to wash my hand

At the waters' edge where I wet my feet

Is such a treat

96

As it rains we sit and watch

The streaming of the rain drops

Moisture it leaves on the ground

Help in many ways all around

97

Pen in hand one thinks to write

But what sense will one derive

Verses that are mild and mellow, and not trite

Will at times survive

98

Speech comes easy for some men

While others struggle to no end

Some are polite and quite soft-spoken

While others shout with speech broken

99

When sadness comes into your heart

Love and happiness can tear it apart

It might take time to redeem

Happiness can be nearer than it may seem

100

The road you travel may be rough

But keep on walking, avoid the rut

If you tire just rest awhile

At the end you might feel worn out

Success was yours, you finished the mile

101

We should always say a prayer

Not just for some but for everyone

Give us strength to love each other

To live our life like one brother

Free us from our selfish ways

So that we can live and just care

102

Have a heart with only goodness

To treat your fellowmen with kindness

Love this earth that is given us

And protect it from the very worst

For it really should matter

To those before us and after

103

Some men lie, mislead, and deceive

While others follow and believe

Promises made are often hollow

Some never care, they still follow

104

A selfish man strives for paradise

With help from others he reaches his goal

Once there he is in heaven

Leaving others to live in hell

105

Man tells lies as if they're true

They're his way to convince you

Telling the truth gives him no gain

Power, control, or needed fame

106

We watch the stars in awe and wonder

Some are alone, some in clusters

Only at night in all their splendor

We experience stars in nature

107

One will never cease to learn

No matter when or where he may roam

The universe has more than we know

For us to learn as we grow

108

As we grow old we enjoy leisure

The young seek nothing but pleasure

Young or old we have a choice

To live at our own desire

The life we know is not forever

109

Don't worry about what was yesterday

Think about a better tomorrow

Make yourself happy in every way

Don't drown yourself in idle sorrow

110

Be happy with the little you have

Don't be ashamed and sad with guilt

What is yours is your very own

And that you shall always have to keep

111

Anything gained by honest means

Makes for one happy being

Bringing joy to your very soul

Adding strength to your ego

112

As we pray for things we need

It should lead us to do our good deed

Prayers answered in many ways

Can make for us better days

While we receive that which we ask

Kindness should be our daily task

113

Heaven is where we hope to be

To enjoy peace and harmony

Hell is never in our wish

That's where sadness and sin exist

We can make our own true heaven

Or choose to live in man-made hell

114

The cock crows, giving his warning

It's time to rise, it's early morning

The dog barks, being alert

Making it known, he is on duty

Rise my friend your tasks await

Times a wasting, don't be late

115

In Spring the grass is fresh and green

Ready to mow and to groom

Hot Summer comes with all its glitter

And all the green will start to wither

Only to rise again next Spring for Summer

116

We know not why we were born

We know not why we have to die

To be informed is to know

Acquire knowledge as you grow

Where things appear to be hidden

Look for answers, it's yours to know

ABOUT THE AUTHOR

Fren Thompson was born and raised in Jamaica, West Indies, and is the fifth and youngest offspring of low-income parents. He grew up in a modest home where sharing was caring, giving was receiving, and being kind to others was being kind to yourself. Fren continued these practices throughout his life thereby exemplifying selflessness, sacrifice, and love. Fren Thompson is also the author of To Find a Place – a tale of exploitation and love.